Printed in the USA
CPSIA information can be obtained
at www.ICGtesting.com
CBHW030725270824
13727CB00038B/627

9 781648 114465